I Kissed the Ground

MEMORIES AND MIRACLES

Kitty Hart

MIEKO PUBLISHING

MIEKO PUBLISHING

Hardcover: 978-1-945505-70-6
Paperback: 978-1-945505-71-3
Ebook: 978-1-945505-72-0

First Edition: June 2023
Printed in the United States of America

10 9 8 7 6 5 4 3 2 1

Contents

As a young child I always had a pull to attend church and pray. But I didn't develop a good bond of spirituality with Jesus until later in life. Many times I should have asked Jesus to be with me, and He was, I just didn't realize it then. The Lord has given me so many blessings and life experiences and miracles to share. It has taken several years to give my heart and soul to the Lord. So with love for our God and my family, I write these words of memories and miracles.

Please know that I am not a writer and forgive my lack of writing skills. This book shares what I have experienced throughout my life. Originally, I intended this to be written for my family only, but it was changed July 6, 2021 because of a remarkable miracle.

After reading my book, some may choose not to believe me or will find a logical explanation of what I have experienced. However, others may embrace it and perhaps, make their faith stronger. Whatever you choose to believe or not, is your own personal decision. I respect that and thank you for reading about my life.

God Bless.

In loving memory of my mom "Ruby"
and for my husband "Jerry"

Early Life (Minnesota)

Looking back, my life seems not to be very odd in the least. It was filled with tears, sadness and lots of confusion. There was an awful lot for my brothers, sisters, and myself to endure. However, there was some happiness at times, especially the love from my mother and siblings.

A little background about my parents. My mother (Ruby) was from the south and had one brother, Bill. They lived part of their life with their mother (my grandmother) Martha Missouri Marcum. Their mom moved to Minnesota and left Ruby and Bill with their grandparents in Alabama.

My Great-Grandmother was a Medicine Woman. She collected herbs and made various kinds of potions for healing. People came to visit her when they were ill. My mom continued doing this and used the remedies on us kids. One of the most unusual remedies I distinctly remember was when I had a bad earache. I was at my mom's home after her funeral. My sister Lela took a newspaper, rolled it up into a cone shape, and placed the small part inside my ear. Then she lit the top and soon after, blew out the flame. Within an instant, little puffs of smoke came out of the top of the newspaper cone. My earache was gone and we all laughed and wondered if our mother's presence was there. She would have been so proud.

My Great-Grandfather was a farmer in the hills, but I'm sorry to say he molested mom (Ruby) while she lived there. My mom would have been about six to nine years old. My poor mother endured a lot but I guess back then, it was quite common and not considered unusual or illegal. My mom only went to school through the fourth grade.

My grandmother Martha was in Minnesota where she became a "Lady of the Night" and had wealthy clients. She eventually brought mom and Bill where she was. My grandmother was a beautiful lady and breast cancer took her life early. I never had the opportunity to meet my grandmother, Martha. Bill died of complications of Parkinson's Disease and my mother died at the age of 89 due to pancreatic and stomach cancer.

Mom did the best she could raising us kids. Her upbringing didn't help prepare her to be a wife and mother. But she figured it out on her own, loved us, and was a very hard worker.

Ruby and her brother, Bill Marcum.

Grandmother, Martha Missouri Grimes

Father, Ed Pekula

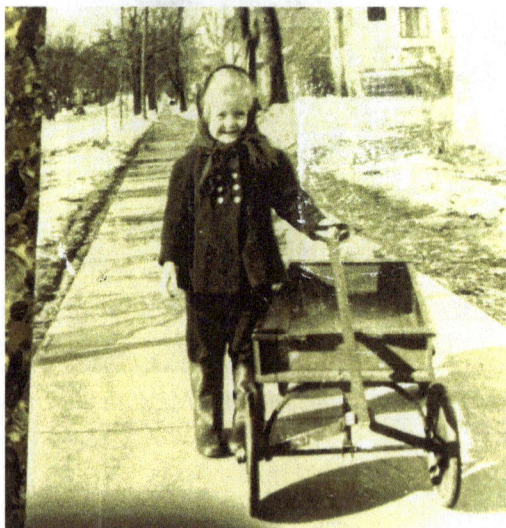

Kitty as a child

My father (Ed Pekula) was one of ten children. His parents were Catholic and came to the United States from Poland. Dad was a tall, good-looking man. Gardening and playing the harmonica were favorites of his. For some reason the song, "You Are My Sunshine" rings a bell for me and has stuck in my mind for all of my years. I always thought I'd like to play the harmonica. Well, that hasn't gone too well. So the harmonica sits in a drawer. Someday I may get it out again and learn to play "You Are My Sunshine."

Unfortunately, my father became an alcoholic. He also loved the ladies. Not a good husband or father. He liked to spend his paychecks at the bar.

Two boys and four girls came from this marriage. The first child died as a baby. I was the youngest. My brother and sisters attended Catholic School. Years later my sisters Shirlee, Nancy, Jan and I revisited our old school, home, and church. It brought back lots of memories for us. I don't remember much about Minneapolis, Minnesota, but I do remember wearing a little red snowsuit with a wagon beside me. I have a picture of me with that wagon!

Years later I would see my paternal grandmother, Katherine. I must have been twelve or so. Getting to finally meet her was an exciting event! I was named after her which made it extra special. I was so excited! I had planned on a huge hug and kisses and hearing her say my name with a Polish accent. But when she saw me she just said "hello" and walked by me. I was totally ignored! Could this be the grandma I always had such love for?? This was to be a real traumatic event and I could not understand her rejection of me. I was crushed. I felt no love for her after that.

I never met Grandfather Andrew. I was told that he was kind, sweet, meek and mild, and talked softly. I've been told I resemble him with my round face and blue eyes.

Grandfather Andrew and Grandmother Katherine

Mom had it really tough supporting all of us kids. Divorce was in the near future and this was to be a sad affair. Denny and Shirlee (my two oldest siblings) were given to my dad and Nancy, Jan, and I were given to my mother. It ended up that dad gave Denny to one of his sisters and he fared quite well. Shirley also was given to a different sister and it was not so good for her as she was passed around and she felt more like a servant. She missed us all badly. Mom sent letters to Shirlee but they were never given to her. Shirlee thought mom did not want her anymore. A terrible time in her life, I can't imagine her sadness.

Catherine Kaiser and Andrew Pikula
on their wedding day, Oct 19, 1897

Josephine (Stanek) Pikula
(1845-1922)
Andrew's mother

9

Josephine Pekula in native dress, early turn of the century, Poland. Andrew Pekula's mother

We eventually moved to St. Peter, Minnesota. Shirlee was able to join us at that time. Soon after, she was married to a farmer named Larry. Denny went into the military. Mom remarried a man named Martin. This was the beginning of hell.

Some traumatic events happened to my sister and me. My stepdad, Martin, raped Nancy several times. He told Nancy if she told our mom, we would be sent to an orphanage and we'd never see our mom again. She was about nine when this started. Mom found out when my sister Jan heard Nancy crying in the barn. She ran to the barn and the door was locked. She got our mom and he was caught in the act! That ended, but I never understood why my mom stayed with him.

I was probably two when Martin would come for me. He put me in his bed and there he would molest me. I was so little, and this would continue for the next two years. As this went on, I developed physical problems that required medical treatment. My mom thought it was me being young and exploring my body, but that was not the case.

The house we moved to was in the country, with an outhouse, no electricity, a water pump in the kitchen and a bucket under the sink. It was a white, two-story house, very creepy and scary. There were lots of trees in the yard and a lake behind. Mom always told us it had quicksand in it to scare us away from the lake. It worked! A vivid memory of mine is looking for my kittens and I happened to look into a well in the front yard. They had all been thrown in. Many tears and sadness for me.

We always got one pair of shoes for school and if we got a hole in the bottom, mom would put in a piece of cardboard to cover it. In the spring, as our shoes got too small, mom would cut the toe out and told us they were sandals. In the summer, we went barefoot. Mom would darn our socks that had holes, making a pattern similar to cross stitch. They looked new to me. I too did this for a time when first married. Imagine some things you carry with you! Soon gave that up!

***

Here is another memory from St. Peter, Minnesota. Mom worked at an "Insane Asylum," as they called it back then. It was a mental institution. This facility was close to our home. Two patients had escaped and were still missing. We kids were home alone and heard a noise upstairs and it scared us. There was a thump, stop, thump, stop. We thought it was the missing patients that had come and got into our house. We hid and huddled, almost in tears, and the noise came nearer. We peeked and it was our puppy dragging a shoe by the shoelace down the stairs! My grandchildren always loved to hear this story and of course, I embellished it and spoke with a spooky voice.

One more humorous story about my sisters, Shirlee and Nancy. They didn't like to get up in the night and use the outhouse. So they would hang their rear-ends out the window. In time, there became a yellow streak from the girls' bedroom window to the bottom of the house! All was well until mom happened to walk around the house and discovered this. They were in big trouble. Mom made a switch from a small tree branch by removing all of the leaves. I guess it was very painful. Needless to say, that was the end of that.

Most of our meals were bacon grease with bread, pickled pig's feet, or perhaps boiled chicken feet. Whatever mom could get cheap or free from the butcher. Many times, she wouldn't eat and said she wasn't hungry. You know, I still remember the taste of chicken feet and it wasn't all that bad. Chewing the meat off those little knuckles was rather quite good! Haven't done that since or cared to.

We lived in five different homes in St. Peter, Minnesota. I attended kindergarten there. One of our homes was an upstairs apartment above a movie theater. Mom worked a few doors down from there as a waitress. My best memory there was finding my love for singing and dancing. So much that I would sing and dance when the drunks came out of the bar next door to our apartment and they would give me money. I was doing quite well until my mom found out. That was the end of my singing and dancing career.

Shantyville (Wyoming)

Mom and Martin were always fighting and yelling. Our home was in chaos much of the time. We kids would hide upstairs, watching and listening through a register. Thankfully, my sisters and I could handle these circumstances together.

After a time, mom left Martin. She called my dad. He told her to come there. We got on a Greyhound bus and moved to Casper, Wyoming, where my dad was. Our leaving was very secretive; even Shirlee did not know. Not sure if mom was afraid and didn't want Martin to know. We had very few belongings with us, and dad was supposed to meet us there. We arrived in the night. No one was there, only three tired kids, very little money, and a very disappointed and upset mother.

Later that night, we found him. He was living with a woman named Francis and her children. I will never forget that night and how as a little child, I hated him so much for that. Never did forgive him or ever got close to him after that.

We found a little one-room shack in Shantyville, as I called it. "Shantyville" consisted of several wooden, one-room shacks and two large outhouses. We had a bed, a table, and four chairs. Nancy, Jan, and I slept on the bed and mom on three chairs all lined up.

Mom got a waitress job which she loved! She was a wonderful waitress, and I had seen her with several plates lined up on her arm and even between her fingers; it was awesome!

Joe came into our lives and shortly after, mom and he were married. Joe drove a bus, and I liked him, but my sisters did not. Maybe because they were older than me as the reason. He told them that he was their boss from now on, and you can imagine how that went over. I was about six, Jan was eleven, and Nancy was fourteen. It is hard for older children to accept a stepfather for several reasons, with control issues for sure. A little brother David and sister Lela joined our family later.

I was fascinated by Joe. He was a cowboy with a western family heritage. We moved around Casper about seven times. At one school I attended, I tried out for a part in an operetta. I got the lead and was so excited. I was to be a princess named Lucy Lacey Lizabell and had a solo to sing. I still remember the song I sang. It was called "Dreamily Rustle." Mom made me a pretty pink dress with white bows on it. The concert was held in a big center in Casper. I must have done well for a fifth grader because after the performance, my mom was approached by talent scouts, and they wanted me to go to New York to study singing and dancing lessons. Who knows, maybe I could have been another Shirley Temple, but mom said no. No one was taking her girl away.

Nancy, my sister and her boyfriend Roger took Jan and me Jack Rabbit hunting one night when she was stuck with us. Oh, so much fun riding around crazy in a jeep in the boonies of the sand brush, chasing rabbits in the beam of a spotlight! Nancy threatened me if I ever told mom, and I didn't.

Jan had a couple of jobs working in a movie theater as an usher. An usher would show you to your seat at that time while holding a flashlight. She also worked in a drugstore, and all her salaries had to be given to my folks except for a few dollars.

Seemed like my only job was to babysit Dave and Lela. Usually, I would push them in a stroller and sing to them.

I attended Catholic School for one year. I thought the nuns were very mean and did not like me. One recess, we girls would twirl around and see whose skirt would go out the farthest. They caught me when it was my turn, and I was in big trouble. At lunchtime, we took our lunch at desks in another classroom. Apparently, I left some breadcrumbs behind. The nuns came into the classroom, yelled at me, and made me clean up my breadcrumbs. I was so embarrassed and cried and cried.

Also, when they called on me to recite a prayer in class, I got so nervous I couldn't say it even though I knew it. I think they picked on me because my parents couldn't afford to donate extra money. I don't know why I was sent there, my parents couldn't afford it, and it was a terrible year for me.

We moved for the seventh time to Casper. Our last move was into a train car remodeled into a home in the country. How ugly it was. Jan was embarrassed by it. We had a horse, and I remember Denny getting bucked off. My mom was screaming, and I was laughing. He had it coming. The minute he got on it, he started kicking the horse. The horse was eventually sold right after that incident.

I was interested in rocks and collected some for a few years. Seems like I lost a few each time we moved. Mom tried to make the load lighter when we moved because I was always missing some. While living there in the country, it was all sand, sagebrush, rocks, and rattlesnakes. I walked out quite a ways until I found a bunch of rocks piled up and started digging. Now that I think about it, perhaps it was a miracle that I never got bit by a rattlesnake.

At the school I attended we played jacks (check that out) but used a golf ball to replace a rubber ball. It had more bounce! Marbles was another favorite of mine and I was pretty good. I accumulated quite a few prized marbles that I had won. Jumprope, hopscotch, tag and Red Rover were also favorites. I loved paper dolls and coloring books. In the winter I played Fox and Geese, had snowball fights and build snow forts.

Nighttime Visitor (Nebraska)

Nancy was now married to Roger and free from her unhappy life. Jan soon moved in with Nancy in Casper. Later, Jan got married to Paul, who was in the Air Force.

Again the packing began, and we headed to Omaha, where Denny was. This time I cried my eyes out. We had a big dog, and we just drove away and left him on the steps to wait for us. How cruel was that! My poor dog! Later, we found out that a nest of rattlesnakes was close to our home. This area was known for rattlesnakes.

During the long drive to Omaha, it was my job to keep Dave and Lela entertained on the trip. So I sang all the way, songs they liked such Little Red Caboose, Three Little Fishes, Bill Gowens Goat, Bunny Bed, and so on. I still sing them to myself from time to time to just get a kick out of it!

We moved three times while we lived in Omaha. Our first home was in a predominantly African-American neighborhood. I was always friendly, but my classmates did not like me and would always say, "Stay away, white girl." I was very lonely and sad. It was my birthday, and I thought if I had a birthday party, maybe some of them would come and become my friends. Not one showed up.

I moved to another house that I liked. It was across from Hanscom Park in Omaha. There was a beautiful Catholic

Church on the other side. I could finally go to church every Sunday. Just me, my little hat on my head, and my missal book! The mass was in Latin, and I could follow along with what was going on with my book because it had pictures.

I had to walk across this huge park, and I have no idea why someone didn't try to abduct me. Perhaps another miracle. While living in this home, my parents were extremely poor. I heard them talking one night; they were so worried about food and their bills. Mom told Joe she had a jar of loose coins to take to the bank in the morning. Hearing that made me worry. I was about eleven years old. I went upstairs and lay down with my brother and sister on a mattress on the floor. Laying there, I started saying my prayers and telling God how worried I was about my parents. As I was praying, the room lit up and began to glow. In front of me, at the end of the mattress, was the hazy shape of an angel. I could tell it was a female, beautiful, but not clear. Enough to know what I was seeing. I couldn't say a word but felt so calm and such peace. I received a message in my mind, "Do not be afraid; it will be OK." Then she slowly faded away. I thought this was normal and never told Mom or anyone else for years.

Mom, Dave, Lela, and I went to the bank the next morning. The kids and I went into a corner, waiting while mom was in line. For some reason, I looked down, and there lay a $20 bill! I showed her and will never forget her words. In a whisper, my mom said, "Where did you get that?" I told her and showed her that no one was around us. Well, we left right there with her jar in hand. Groceries were bought, and some bills were paid. Thank you, God, for answering my prayers! Twenty dollars back then was worth about $220 today.

I have read some books and articles on angels visiting children. Most of the time, they appear at the end of the bed. But children were not afraid and did not tell of their experiences until later in life, as I have.

Love for an Old Man (Idaho)

Joe was always good to me, and I was fascinated with his western heritage. I was very fond of him. He was from Idaho, and that is where his family lived. It was at this time that we moved to Idaho to help Joe's father, who was ill. His name was William "Bill" Rusk, and his wife, Polly. They lived in Leadore, Idaho. A very small town, at one time, had old dusty sidewalks and painted wooden buildings, almost right out of a western movie. Lewis and Clark and Sacagawea had been in this area at one point in history. All of this is right up my alley! Cowboys, mountains, horses, antelope…it couldn't have been any better. I loved it there!

Bill was my grandpa in every sense of the word. He told me of his life, including cowboying and driving a stagecoach. I would hang on to every word and imagine the scenes he described. He always called me "My Girl." I loved to sing and dance for him all around his bed when he became bedridden. I sure believed he loved it, and I did as well. Grandpa was 90 when he passed; I loved that old man very much and cried my heart out. Bill was blind.

After Bill's death, we lived in Salmon, Idaho. Very picturesque, a typical western town. I adored Joe's brother, Ray. He was a true cowboy, too, and had many cowboy jobs. He also panned for gold. He bought me a beautiful pair of moccasins, which I wore the life out of! Joe also had a sister named

Grace, and her husband was Oliver. They raised mink and other animals. They used the pelts to create purses, hats, etc., which were very beautiful. They also made clocks from burl wood. (Burls are large growths on trees.)

While living in Salmon, I loved visiting the saddle shop to see saddles made. I loved the smell of the leather. Life couldn't get any better there. At times in the winter I would walk out to the frozen creeks and pretend to ice skate all the while watching the antelope and deer up on the mountain-side and valley before me. What a wonderful sight! I really loved Idaho!

Joe and mom bought a restaurant and bar called the Silver Spur. Mom worked her butt off as a waitress. Not sure what Joe did unless he cooked or bartended. They sent for my sister Jan to come to help out. They started having financial problems, and soon they would lose their restaurant. After that, there were lots of arguments and fighting. I would be so scared and try to get between them during their fights and then lay on the end of mom's bed, worrying that they would start all over again. What a chaotic life for a little girl in sixth grade. After living in three homes in Salmon, we left for another little town called Mackay, Idaho. Joe started a trash-hauling business, and mom was a waitress.

I made some friends, and we loved riding bikes. It was fun to attach playing cards to the spokes of the wheel to make it sound like a motorcycle. It was in Mackay that I saw an old woman waving at me as I rode by on my bike. I would wave back. Finally, I stopped one day and we sat on her porch visiting, and she would bring out cookies. This would go on for many days after. I just loved to hear all the stories she told. I wish I could remember her name. Don't know why, but I have always been drawn to older people.

It was there that I heard my first rock and roll music; I was hooked and fell in love with it! During that time, my creative mind led me to put on shows for parents and anyone we could get to come.

I would enlist the talents of my friends and my brother Dave. He would dress like Davy Crockett, and I sang that song and most of the others. By the way, we sold kool-aid! What fond memories. I came home one day to find mom crying and the refrigerator being repossessed. Well, that meant one thing, on the road again. So we packed up again, and I said goodbye to my friends.

Best Friend (Iowa)

What I remember about our trip to Omaha was that I had forgotten about all the trees, and as we got closer, it was so green. It was also the first time I saw television. I was in seventh grade.

After living in five different homes, we moved to Carter Lake, Iowa. I liked living in Carter Lake! I had a best friend, Cheryl, and we are still friends today. I began to notice boys then, but they did not notice me. I was such a skinny minnie then. We had a junior high dance, and no boy asked me to dance. Darn! So I danced with the other girls.

The school play was to be in the spring, and I tried out for it. I was lucky and got the leading part. It was so exciting, and I was oh so happy! That is until the music teacher wanted me to dye my blonde hair black. Mom said, "Absolutely not," and that was that. Later, however, I sang a duet with my friend at our eighth-grade graduation.

A church was allowed to have services at my school. ,At that time, I accepted the Lord as my savior. Something had moved me to do this.

My churchgoing ended abruptly. One of the young leaders took a bunch of us kids for a picnic and some games at a park. One of the games involved swinging us around, then dropping us and remaining in the pose that you fell in. The game was called Statue. He swung me around, holding onto my breasts. It scared me and I found out that's what he did to another girl, too. I was more surprised and saddened than mad to believe that I was so trusting in him.

Mom raised rabbits in our backyard. They were so cute, but for some reason, one by one, they would disappear. She would give us a reason, and of course, I believed my mom.

One really bad rainy day, I was walking to school which was several blocks away. A car stopped beside me. The driver was a man who asked if I needed a ride. I was so trusting I said yes. Fortunately, he took me to school. I was stupid to do that. Maybe he was an angel; perhaps that was another miracle, as this could have turned out really bad.

Black Eye (Nebraska)

Again, my folks decided we needed to move back to Omaha, and we did. Here we go again. I had a couple of good friends there. I traded in my leather fringe coat and boots for a black imitation leather coat and saddle shoes. We wore bobby socks with really thick tops. We had lots of fun, sockhops, movies, roller skating, friends, and parties, all great fun. The dances included: Jitterbug, Chicken, Stroll, Mashed Potatoes, and slow dancing without our bodies touching. We wore crinolines, which were layers of stiff netting under our skirts. When they got a little limp, we would make sugar water, dip the netting in it, and spread it out flat in a circle until it dried. Good ole rock and roll days!

I did meet my first boyfriend there and had my first real kiss. He was a good kisser! I was not allowed to date until I was 16. I could only sit on the front steps with him. He was really cute and wore his hair in a waterfall and ducktail. You may have to look that one up someday. His name was Johnny.

I attended Tech High School in Omaha for my first year. It was a very tough neighborhood, and many race riots occurred. White gangs, African-Americans, Hispanics, etc., always fought after school. No guns, thank God for that! I was always afraid and had a very long walk to school.

This was to be the worst year of school I ever had. While walking through the halls, I would sometimes be shoved or get my butt pinched. I never had it in my bones to fight. I was so timid and never wanted any conflict. I saw many kids pushed inside lockers or put in trash cans and sent rolling down a flight of stairs. No one ever tried to stop this, and it was so sad.

For whatever reason, I attracted an east Omaha gang of girls. This was not going to be good. Probably because I was timid, and that is what bullies like, so they chose me. I was scared all of the time.

Back then, we had PE clothes to change into for that class. I would often return, and my clothes would be in the toilet. They loved that and laughed their heads off. Or I would be on the track running, and someone would stick their foot out and trip me. Not only did it hurt, but I was also scared, embarrassed, and traumatized.

I tried talking to a counselor there and was told they couldn't help me, mostly because it was only threats.

One day after school, I crossed the street on my way home. There they were, waiting for me. As I got closer, they formed a circle around me and started shoving me from one to another while screaming at me. I remember sobbing until I finally started swinging and hitting with my fists. It went downhill from there. I got knocked down, and I lay there. No one would help me. They said, "If we ever see you again, we will cut you up like a dirty rat." I will never forget those words.

The school called mom later and told her what had happened, and said they couldn't do anything because it was not on the school property. I said shame on them for not helping me. For me, it was nothing more serious other than bruises, cuts, a black eye, and trauma.

I've often wondered if these now-grown women ever think of me and are sorry for what they did. Probably not.

Happy Memories (Iowa)

Lucky for me, and a tremendous relief, when we moved to Pisgah, Iowa. My folks bought a cafe and bar. I loved that little town. As we drove down between a couple of hills, it looked so beautiful nestled at the bottom. Living there was the best time of my life! I lived there for two years and moved twice in that town of 400-500 people. I would always call Pisgah my hometown!

The business was a lot of hard work for my parents, and I would help as much as possible. Sometimes if mom didn't need me, I detasseled corn. Oh, what a hot and dirty job. Sometimes when pulling out the tassels, worms would fall on me. I also walked beans and would get so sunburned. I was now a sophomore in high school.

There was a school carnival that fall. I was chosen to be the queen, and I needed a dress. We were still very poor so mom and I went to the Goodwill in Omaha to shop. I found an apricot-colored strapless dress with netting. Not really that great, but nonetheless, all we could afford and the best we could do. All was fine and well, until a teacher remarked that she did not like my dress and was very critical of it. I never figured that out, but I can still see her embarrassing me. I was hurt but knew that although my dress was not pretty, it was all my parents could afford. I was too timid to say anything back to the teacher.

Since I loved to sing, I was involved with choir, sextets, trios, etc. My best friend Pat and I would do lots of duets. Pat and I also loved to dance and would do so at the jukebox at my folk's cafe.

Never really played basketball before Pisgah, but I grew to love it. I did not make the team my sophomore year, but I went to every practice they had and became the student manager.

The next year I made the second string and I was so proud. My hard work paid off. My best memory was a game that I went in as a forward. I also played guard. We only played half-court, three on each side, and you could only take two dribbles and either pass or shoot. So I went in, and by sheer luck, I made a basket. Well, those two points helped win the game! I was called "Two-Point Kitty" for a while, my only claim to fame.

At the sports dinner, the coach talked about me and my determination to play the game when I wasn't on the team. I felt like a million bucks.

My parents did not attend any of my games or programs, nor did they attend any of my siblings' activities. I understood how busy they were because they worked. So I would attend Lela and Dave's programs and Dave's Boy Scout functions. I took them with me to church. I tried taking them to the Catholic Church first, but they liked the Methodist Church best because of Sunday School. I would go to the Catholic Church when I could.

Seemed like I was a mother to my siblings rather than a sister. When they were sick in the night, I took care of them. I did all of the babysitting. It couldn't be helped, but it sure did interfere with my social life. Just glad to be there and help out.

My First Love (Iowa)

Pisgah is where I was to meet my husband, Jerry Carrier. He was a little James Dean, Clint Eastwood, and Charles Bronson all rolled up into one. He was very good-looking and tough. Jerry had a really cool 1959 red Ford Galaxie 500 jacked up in the back, white fur around the rearview mirror, a pair of big fur dice hanging off the mirror, and silver fender skirts. Talk about a beauty!

Friends told me to stay away from him as he was wild. Well, that only made him more exciting. Too late; I was already in love. We did a lot of drag racing and playing chicken with the cars, usually on a desolate highway. When you play chicken, you go down the middle of the highway, two cars racing toward each other. The first one to swerve was the chicken. Lord, it is a wonder that we weren't all killed.

We also had fun stealing watermelons. The farmers were not happy when we would sneak into their patches. When we knew the melons were ripe, we would grab a couple and run. Then we would drop one in the middle of the road, and oh boy, it tasted so good as we each ate a chunk with the juice running down our arms.

Jerry told the story of when he was young and waiting for the Coke truck to drive up the steep hill on the country road. This is when the bottles would be in crates on open truck beds. Well, he and his friend Russell and other buddies would wait until he showed up, driving slowly up the steep hill and riding their horses from behind the trees. They would each grab a bottle off of the truck, leaving the driver yelling and waving his arms. Oh, for the fun of the good old days! I always loved that story.

Jerry gave me the money to buy a prom dress when I was a junior in school. It was so beautiful, light blue, ruffles, and strapless. I had a little bit of a hard time keeping it up. I bought some plastic heels and a purse. I felt like a princess even though I was really skinny. We went steady for six months, and he gave me a diamond that Christmas. I really fell hard for him.

My folks lost the restaurant in Pisgah. However, shortly after that, the cafe was known as The Filler Up and Keep on Trucking Cafe. The Old Home bread commercial used ads with CW McCall as the trucker. Mavis was the waitress.

Our next move took us back to Omaha. Jerry picked me up on our wedding day (June 16, 1960). This is crazy but we had no marriage plans. We just picked the date and went to the courthouse in Logan, Iowa with his parents, Fred and Juanita, my mom, and also Dave and Lela, my brother and sister. We drove around Logan until we found a minister that would marry us. No flowers, no pictures, but we were oh so happy! I felt sorry for Jerry because his parents would not go for our wedding vows. I don't think Juanita approved of me and rightly so because we were so young. This was not what she had planned for her son. Jerry was nineteen and I was seventeen. We honeymooned in Okoboji for a few days.

Jerry and I would live our married life in five different homes in Mondamin, Iowa. I was a senior in high school and missed my first semester. I had promised my mom I would finish high school. Jerry's mom (a grade school teacher) persuaded the high school principal to let me finish school. I was allowed to finish the last semester because I doubled up on classes, read books, and reported on them. I did it, but it was very hard.

School was always difficult for me, partly because of the moving. However, I was able to earn Cs and an occasional B. I loved English and History. Math and Typing were awful. Maybe this is why I wrote this book in longhand!

***

I was seventeen and a new wife. I was the first married student who attended that high school. Jerry then worked at a gas station and I worked at a hardware store until I started school. I also worked during Christmas vacation. Life was very hard then, but it was the life that I had chosen. We were so poor I would pick up pop bottles to sell. We lived in a small home with tar paper around the foundation and plastic over the windows. It was so cold that washcloths would freeze in the bathroom, and pipes would freeze under the house. We did not have a washer or dryer then, so I used a scrubboard. I remember Jerry or me crawling under the house with a torch to unthaw the frozen water pipes. I often had to open the oven door and turn it on to keep us warm. So much for the good old days.

Our first daughter Cyndi was born two years later. She was very colicky, and I cried about as much as she did. Julie arrived on Cyndi's birthday two years later in the tiny, cold house we lived in. Six years later, Lyn joined our family.

By then, we had three daughters, Cyndi, Julie, and Lyn. I was still a churchgoer, but Jerry did not want them to be Catholics for whatever reason. So I chose the Methodist Church, where I taught Sunday School and Vacation Bible School. The girls were baptized at that time.

On the hot, humid summer days, the kids spent much time playing in the sprinkler. I also gave the girls cool baths, then laid them on a sheet in the living room to play or nap. A small oscillating fan was our lifesaver. Seems like we either froze in the winter or suffocated in the summer.

Our next home was on a very small acreage, and we raised alfalfa for our horses. Always had two around and maybe a pony. Horses and playing cards with our friends Myrna and Gordon were our favorite pastimes. Their three kids were about the same ages as our kids. I remember buying one six-pack of pop that all ten of us shared. Kids, food, and horses were our top priorities then.

So Young, Too Young (Iowa)

Married life for Jerry and me was bittersweet. I cried an awful lot, and Jerry did not talk to me for weeks at a time, but we were both young and teenagers. No wonder we had lots of problems! I was timid and would not speak up for myself, and Jerry was so jealous. It took years, and we finally learned lessons about life and marriage.

I often wondered if Jerry wished he would have listened to his friend, who offered to help pay for Veterinary School. Jerry was so in tune with animals, especially horses and their care. But he gave that all up for me. Many times if a neighboring vet could not travel to our town, he would tell them to call Jerry Carrier.

There were many wonderful memories of Jerry getting me some wild plum blossoms he picked alongside the road. I loved that so much; better than a bouquet of roses!

One year, Jerry bought me a windmill for Christmas, the best gift I had ever received. We put his grandpa's wagon in front of it. Flowers filled the wagon bed in the summer and in winter, we had lights on the windmill. A cowboy Santa was sitting on the wagon seat. Either season was a sight to behold.

Another Christmas, I'd asked for an electric can opener. Being the prankster he was, he got a hand-held opener that he connected to a wire and plug. Only he would think of that. Good thing I didn't plug it in!

In the winter, he would pull the kids on the tube behind the tractor in the snow. He also made a skating pond for the girls, and they laughed at me because of my wobbly ankles. Our dog, Herman, loved playing on the ice pond with them. We would make snow angels, snowball fights, and forts in the snow. In the summer, Jerry would give the kids a ride on the tractor or a ride on the horse with him. Life was good then.

I had a mare; her name was Katie. She was a beautiful Palomino, and she had a colt. It wasn't breathing when it was born, so Jerry gave the colt mouth-to-mouth. The colt lived. We raised several colts and enjoyed going to horse shows, and had our fair share of ribbons and trophies. Our girls also rode in horse shows.

Saturday nights before the horse shows, we washed down the ones to be shown the next day. We would load up horses, lunch, baby bottles, and kids the day of the show. Lots of work for sure, but that was our enjoyment. We showed our horses. Myrna and Gordon went with us since they showed their horses, too.

We did not have a pasture but a dry lot instead . So that meant lots of horse manure to scoop out every Saturday and then use the manure spreader on our alfalfa fields.

Cutting and bailing the alfalfa three to four times a year was quite a job. Bales were heavy, but I managed to drive the tractor, throwing bales, or stacking them in the shed. I was once a tough country woman!

One of my favorite memories was of the big garden we had. We had every imaginable vegetable possible. We had huge strawberry beds and raspberry plants. I did a lot of freezing and canning. I cooked beets outside on a roaster. After they had cooled, I would peel and eat many right there, and I loved it! I probably peed pink for about a week.

Cyndi was good at horseback riding and showing. Once we thought she might be a good jockey because of her expertise and size. That did not happen, but she enjoyed all the beautiful horses she had.

I remember when we brought a new horse for our daughter, Julie. My mare, Katie, kicked at the new horse, and Julie, who was in the yard alone then, happened to be in the way. We heard a scream, and all of us ran out. Not taking time to open the gate, Jerry just took off running and jumped over a five-foot fence. I couldn't believe my eyes, and I was right behind him and decided to go through the gate. I went crazy, grabbed her from his arms and ran to the car. Threw Julie into the backseat, got into the driver's seat, and Jerry yelled at me that he would do the driving. I bailed over the front seat and landed on Julie. She was OK but carried the print of a horseshoe on her chest for quite a while. Guess I'm not good in a crisis!

Lyn started out riding by herself at an early age, around 4 years. She wanted to ride every morning, so we would go into the lot, saddle her pony, Sweetie, and she would ride around the lot. I would just sit on the ground daydreaming until she once said, "Mommy, I can do handstands on Sweetie." She was starting to stand up on Sweetie's back, which scared me to death. I never moved so fast.

Our beloved Sweetie had to be put down. Our friend dug a large hole, and we had the vet euthanize her. Jerry led her down to the bottom that was to be her grave. This was the hardest thing that he'd ever done. Our sadness lasted quite a while. We had many years of riding Sweetie with our kids and grandkids.

After the kids were older and lost interest in the horses, we bought a two-horse gooseneck trailer with room for tack and hay at the back with the horses. At the front, there was room for a mattress on top; it had a few kitchen cupboards and a port-a-potty. Also had a sink and a small kitchen table. We heated water for showers with a solar bag, which would be placed on the pickup hood in the sun. Then we would get in the back of the trailer where the horses had stood, and hang up the solar bag, which had a hose and shower head. Felt so good!

We traveled to different places with our friends. Wonderful campfires and stories accompanied our stacking of empty beer cans. One time a buffalo came in through our camp, so we slowly moved out of the way and hid behind big trees.

Sure were some beautiful rides. One of our friends was Larry, and we enjoyed him so much. He always brought baby powder along for his tush. Once in a while, little white puffs would come from his backside; we sure teased him. Don't think he ever lived that one down.

Jerry enjoyed hunting deer and pheasant. He would go up into the hills where he used to live. He would sit very still under a tree, quietly waiting for a deer. Then out would come inquisitive rabbits and birds. They would come right up to him. He got a big kick out of that. He was looking forward to taking grandkids out someday.

My love for dancing got us into country western dancing. I bought a dance tape and convinced him to try it. He was not too happy about that, but finally, we practiced in the house and front deck. Hey, we weren't too bad! We went to our first dance with our friends, and that's all it took. Our favorite band was called Competition, in which our friend, Dave, played. And we followed them all over.

Jerry was still quite a prankster, along with his best friend, Mel. He and his co-workers were always playing jokes on each other. A few of many were when we bought a small camper and parked it by our shed. I came home from work, and in its place was a crappy old camper with a bucket in front called a "port-a-pot." There were two broken-down chairs and a ratty old grill nearby. Pretty good, huh!

I may come home to a chicken tied up by the leg to a tree. Our yard was looking like death valley with various bones laid out like cattle died in their tracks on a cattle drive, with various skulls and bones on our deck or in the grill.

On Christmas one year, we woke up in the morning to Christmas trees everywhere in our yard. I think Jerry's friends placed an ad stating "Jerry and Kitty Carrier will accept all old Christmas trees."

It wasn't unusual for me to stop at the Jiffy Mart for a few groceries. I would come out to find my car filled completely with cardboard grocery boxes. I'd have to remove them all before I could get in the car to leave.

I could write an entire book about the pranks Jerry and his friends played on me!

We eventually found a hobby we both enjoyed in the winter: making different things out of horseshoes, stirrups, anything western, tack and such. Also, we made clocks out of wood, painting unusual pieces, and painted anything from pigs, horses, tractors, on the wood. The wood had to cure for several weeks. We used walnut, maple, burlwood (large growths from tree trunks). Jerry would burn into the wood first and then I would paint the pictures. We started going to craft shows with our wares and did quite well. We also sold and took orders for Dick's Western Store in Omaha. This was both rewarding and fun.

The coating we put on was a hard lacquer; it became a hard clear covering. Jerry would take a little hand torch and heat it and melt it on the top. That process would bringing air bubbles to the top. It is beautiful when dry, but until then, we had to be careful because anything—even as small as an eyelash—could ruin the piece.

In the fall, Jerry started acting odd, he would be very tearful at one moment and then another moment, be like a raging bull. Very unsettling and scary. I began to think it might be the product that we were using. I contacted the company and that was it. We had been using it in a closed room, where it should have been used in a ventilated room. It affected his central nervous system and he could have died. We stopped immediately and he began to recover. We were so stupid but didn't want to mar the final coating.

Jerry and Kitty

Troubled Times (Iowa)

Jerry suffered a heart attack early spring. Thank God he recovered. We had to change our eating habits and he had to do a lot of walking. Our long driveway was rock, not the best to walk on with boots. He never wore anything but boots. To his dismay, he had to buy tennis shoes. He griped every time he put them on and never wore them after he recovered. Didn't matter where we were, a beach in the Bahamas, he still wore his boots and swimming trunks. That's just the way he was.

Two of our daughters were married by now. Cyndi and Greg had three sons: Kellen, Kyle, and Klint. Julie and Terry, had one daughter Jillian. Lyn, our youngest, was soon to be married to Brian, and their daughter Erin followed a few years later.

Years before, Jerry worked really hard one summer spraying chemicals on crops. He would always come home wet and reek of the scent of chemicals on his body and clothes. In those days, we didn't realize the consequences of that spraying. He was trying to earn the money to buy an air conditioner. He also was in charge of anhydrous ammonia. A couple large tanks were right across from our house. One night, it was leaking quite badly and he went over to find the leak. The air was so bad, you could hardly breathe and it made your eyes tear. I never saw him wear a mask. I couldn't figure out why. Perhaps back then, masks were not used. No wonder he would die at an early age.

Jerry hadn't been feeling well and had tests done. He was going downhill fast. I remember him coming home, his head down and he was so sad. He told me his diagnosis, inoperable esophageal cancer and was given one year to live. We just hung onto each other and cried and cried. It was tough to keep this a secret from our daughters. Lyn was to be married in a week and we waited to tell the girls until Lyn came back from her honeymoon.

Doctors suggested surgery to move his stomach up under his ribs to perhaps give him more months to live, which was excruciating for him. Jerry and I were told that this would extend his life much longer and he would have better days. Little did we know, before surgery, he was having his better days. But we kept hoping and praying. He was now on a feeding tube, and bouts of various other problems were taking a toll. We knew the inevitable; he was always in so much pain.

Jerry worked as long as he could. He worked as a general manager of the co-op at that time. There was a retirement party planned for him with his favorite band and a dance. Jerry was always begging me to sing with the band so I called our friend Dave. He was the leader and I asked if I could sing a couple songs with them. No one knew this, so that night I went to the ladies room to wait.

Dave told Jerry, "Jerry, we have a special surprise for you. A new singer is added to our band." So out I walked and Jerry looked so happy and was laughing, my girls were in shock, and my sons-in-law looked like they wanted to crawl under the table. I sang two songs, Mountain Music by Alabama, and Fishin in the Dark by the Nitty Gritty Dirt Band. Both were his most favorites. I did OK I guess. I was asked to come up and sing again. This would be the last time our family laughed and danced together. That one night we could forget what sadness was to come. Dave played *Fishin in the Dark* at dances in tribute to Jerry after that.

I worked for an eye doctor in Onawa and his name was Harry. He and his wife, Jane, became friends of mine. Jerry knew his cancer was incurable and before he died, he drove me around Onawa looking for a house to buy so I wouldn't have to drive on the snowy roads. Our long lane always drifted shut in the winter. I told him no, as my home was in Mondamin. Jerry would sit on the porch and wave to me as I left for work. I cried all the way to work, then cried all the way back home, then gave him a kiss as he sat waiting for me.

He became unable to sleep in our bed because of the pain so he slept in his recliner and I in mine. Sometimes the only relief from pain was when I would rub the bottoms of his feet. I have learned that it is called reflexology. Certain areas of the feet pertain to different areas of the body. That really worked so I continued until he could sleep.

Days passed and he was gravely ill. Jerry asked to be baptized. He started attending church with me while ill, as long as he was able. He believed in Christ. I was happy to have our pastor come to our home to baptize Jerry. Jerry liked the pastor a lot because Jerry could relate to him. At Easter, he wasn't able to go anymore. He asked me to read various readings about Easter in the Bible and we prayed.

Our life with Jerry's mother was difficult. Fred, Jerry's dad, was a sweet man and I loved him very much. He had some nerve problems which continued until his death. Juanita, Jerry's mom, was very controlling and would belittle him in front of others. I felt very sorry for him.

Juanita used to tell of her Aunt Arlie who was so crabby you couldn't stand to be around her. Juanita would say about Aunt Arlie, "If I start acting that way, just bonk me in the head."

Many times Jerry would tell me "Well it's time to get out the ball bat!"

She was angry and hateful at me one time or another and with her family, talking terribly about her sisters, brothers, and their families. I don't think they realized how much she would put them all down. When she would say negative things about the family, Jerry and I always defended them.

During Jerry's heart attack and cancer, she was not supportive. Poor Jerry. It would have been good for her to spend time with him. Even being only a block away, she rarely visited or comforted him in any way.

After his death, she made my life miserable in so many ways. My children and grandchildren were always so good to her. But she soon turned on them also. Then her family also argued with us or ignored us. How Jerry would have been so disappointed with all of his family then. Because of her and her lying, she robbed my daughters of a relationship with Jerry's family. How sad that one woman could have so much control! She could have had so much love from her son, myself, and our family. I only hope that someday Jerry's family realizes that she was so wrong about what she said about all of us. She was not the devoted mother or sister they thought.

Our Life Has Changed (Iowa)

We had to look at tombstones, and that was the hardest thing I ever had to do. He picked out the tombstone, and after his death I had a drawing we had done together of us both riding our horses to put on his tombstone.

Days later I could tell he was starting to disconnect from our world and to begin his journey to Heaven. His eyes had a distant look to them now. One day, he told me to open the back door as his dad was there (Fred had been deceased for quite some time.) I went to the door and told Jerry that he wasn't there and would be coming at a later time. A few days later, Jerry said again, "Dad and Harlan are at the front door." Harlan, Jerry's uncle, was more like a brother and was also deceased. Again, no one was there and I said they would be here later.

My daughters took time to spend nights with me. Julie only lived a short distance from me. His mother lived nearby too. Cyndi was in Pender, Nebraska, and Lyn in Council Bluffs, Iowa.

The night of Jerry's passing, Cyndi had left and Lyn arrived. He was a little restless and then calmed down and was in a very sound sleep. Finally, he could rest without pain.

Where are you, Lord? (Iowa)

Later in the night, I heard a sound that I recognized that death might be near. I contacted the hospice nurse and she said that could last quite a while or even a day. The sound became worse. I called Julie, Juanita, and Cyndi. I knew it would soon be his time. Lyn was crying and screaming at our Lord to end his suffering and pain. I was holding his hand and I told him, "Honey, it is OK to go to Heaven." I saw a trickle of a tear come from his left eye, then slowly he opened his eyes and looked up towards the ceiling. Raised both arms up, then he was gone. At that moment, I felt the room was full of people and this would not be the first time I felt this way. The darndest sensation. Lyn told me later, she felt this also. I quickly called Cyndi before she left. I never will forgive myself that I didn't call her sooner to be with her dad.

He rests high on a hill in a cemetery near Pisgah, Iowa. He died in May 1997 at the age of 56 and I was 54. We had been married nearly 38 years.

Disappointment (Iowa)

It was very difficult and I was lonely after losing Jerry. I lived at the edge of town and remembered going out and screaming at God. I'm sure a lot of people can relate to this after the loss of a loved one.

My children and grandchildren were a great comfort to me. At Christmas I didn't feel like putting up a tree or decorating. My family had different ideas and so it did happen. My mom came and spent Christmas Eve with me, God Bless her, she really loved Jerry as he did her.

I never did understand this, but after Jerry died, pretty much all of our friends seemed to abandon me. At least I felt that way. My kids would ask, "Mom, do you have any plans for the weekend?" Always, the answer was no. So they would take turns doing something with me. I hated that they made changes for me, they had their own families and where were my friends? No one came to visit or call, or ask me to come over. One good friend of ours did ask me to come for supper one night, but when his wife came home with groceries, she was not happy to find me there. I felt sorry for him, he was just trying to do a friendly gesture and I was so embarrassed.

We had a large lot by the road a little ways from the house. I kept it mowed but there were several tree branches that needed to be trimmed. I drove my pickup there, stood in the back with a handsaw and loppers. All was well until another friend saw me and decided he should help. However, I didn't really need it. Again, a wife drives by, sees hubby with me and I am sure he got in trouble when he got home. Funny somehow certain memories stick in your brain.

I love small towns but I found small towns don't love a widow or at least me, they didn't and I surely missed all of my good friends.

Old Market (Nebraska)

Almost a year later, I met Curt Hart. He was a friend of Dr. Harry and his wife Jane. She (Jane) called and asked if I would like to go on a date. What? Me on a date at 55? I could hardly say the word date and told her no. But she said, "He is a really nice man and had lost his wife also."

"OK," I thought, "What is the harm of having dinner with a nice man?"

The date was set for us to to meet at a lovely restaurant in the Old Market in Omaha. When I arrived, there was a man standing at the top of the stairs, I said, "Curt?" and he said, "Kitty?" We had a wonderful meal and he bought me a rose. We had a great conversation and found out we had so much in common.

He asked to take me on a carriage ride after dinner, so we started our ride around the park and suddenly, fireworks started going off. He said he had planned it all for me. I found out later that it was the opening of the park for May Day. He really took advantage of the situation, we always laughed at this.

Our first kiss was that night and this was the beginning of our relationship. So much for just having dinner with a nice man. He drove a convertible and we would drive through my little town. I would duck down so no one would see me as I didn't want to start rumors at that time.

In the meantime, we met each other's family. He proposed and I said yes. Actually I was in love with him first and it took him more time. My son-in-law was Sheriff at that time and he had connections with the police chief in Bellevue and checked Curt out to make sure he was an OK guy. Apparently, he was.

I had an auction and sold my home and moved to Bellevue. I got a job with my former employer, Dr. Harry. It was really tough leaving Mondamin. I cried so hard as I left, leaving so many bittersweet memories.

I loved my job as an optician and I sometimes worked on the doctor's side. I enjoyed the people I worked with a lot. Especially Karen, Emily, Dr. Tom, and Anna. They were helpful and kind. Going from a small town doctor's office to the city was very different and difficult.

When I first met Curt's friends and we would be going out together, the dress code was casual. To me, a nice pair of jeans and top was casual. But I soon learned that was not the case. Curt and I seemed to be playing the roles of country mouse and city mouse a lot.

One more thing on this subject, a friend of Curt's asked me where I was from. I replied, "A small town, Mondamin, Iowa." This friend's response was "How quaint." I really felt belittled and embarrassed. Somehow the word quaint has never had the same meaning for me.

Curt and I talked to our Methodist minister (Bob) and he said we should take compatibility lessons and fill out a questionnaire. We did the test and ended up with both of us writing down the same answers. Guess that meant no classes for us.

We were married August 14, 1999. His son Mark and daughter Missy stood up with him. My three daughters Cyndi, Julie, and Lyn were with me. Curt told me, "Stick with me, Babe, and I will show you the world," and that he has.

Curt's parents were Alvin and Anna Hart. Curt had four brothers and one sister named Mert. The six children, Marvin, Myrtle, Kenneth, Allen, Curt, and Milton. They farmed in Stanton, Iowa. His parents and brother, Milton, were deceased at the time of our courtship.

Curt's first wife, Pat, had passed with cancer about the time of Jerry's death in 1997. Curt and Pat had two children, Mark (married to Tina) and Missi (married to Doug). They have eight grandchildren and eleven great-grandchildren so far.

Home and Happiness (Nebraska)

We bought a condo in Bellevue in a beautiful forested area. We have had the best neighbors and friends here! So many good times and fun. We really enjoy playing water volleyball, and love all of the parties. There are lots of deer, raccoons, and an abundance of birds in the area where we live.

The deer in our neighborhood are truly a joy to watch. From spring with the brand new fawns and their white spotted rumps, playing amongst themselves and running around like little kids. They also play in the sprinklers. They are so cute and the mama deer would just lie down and watch the antics of the babies. But boy do they love to eat our flowers! They just begin to bloom and look so pretty, but soon they are all gone. Ah, such is life, but we really love the deer. They roam freely in our neighborhood, but I sure do miss some of my flowers!

Watching wild turkeys is quite comical. From the gobbles waking us up in the morning to the parade of Toms with their feathers fanned out, trying to attract the hens. In the summer, their babies stay fairly well hidden. But once in a while, you can see a row of them following their mom with their little heads bobbing up and down in the tall grass.

Sometimes when I am walking and the toms are out and about, they would follow me gobbling. I would do the same and gobble back at them. They would all turn their heads at the same time, get excited, and start coming towards me. I don't know what I said to them, but I headed home in a big hurry!

In the fall these crazy turkeys are amazing. Sometimes as many as twenty or more would be on our roofs, mailboxes, cars, porches, railings, and trees. The bad side of this, you have to watch your step or endure the chore of cleaning off your shoes. But I would miss them if they weren't here.

And then there are the raccoons. They love to get up on our bedroom deck and get into the storage totes containing bird feed. Our deck is about 30 feet above the ground. One night I was sleeping and could hear bumping noises. Thinking it was the raccoon, I turned on the porch light and saw six pairs of eyes peeking at me from within our container of seed! They were crying but looked so cute. I took a broom and tried to get them out but they would just hide in the corner and whimper. Finally they figured out how to climb up the broom and took off.

Afterwards we were bombarded with mama and baby racoons on our deck. Tried everything to get rid of them and found the only thing that worked was the hose and spray them with water. That did the trick and I kept it handy by my patio door.

Squirrels that are always trying to sample birdseed are amusing and funny. It is amazing to watch them hang off the bird feeder. We have so many birds and it has given us so much pleasure over the years to watch them. I finally succumbed to using binoculars and reading bird books. Who knows what is next, maybe chasing butterflies with a net!

Curt's sister, Mert became very ill and was in a nursing home. I dearly loved her and this is where another miracle happened. We started taking turns staying at night with her. The night I stayed I held her hand and sang every religious song I knew. I don't have a good voice but it gave me pleasure, nonetheless, to do this for her. Not sure if she enjoyed it though as much as I did.

The afternoon of her death, her children, Curt, and I were there with her. Curt had to leave and it was just her children and me there. The room was bright, blinds open, music on, and the girls were talking. For some reason, I sensed her time was close but she just couldn't let go. I suggested they all go have coffee. I turned off the radio and closed the blinds. I went and sat beside her and held her hand. My words to her were simply, "It's OK to let go. Don (her husband who had already passed) and our Lord are waiting for you, your children will be fine, so don't worry." Within a few seconds she was gone peacefully. Again the room seemed to be filled with other people. I looked around thinking the family or nurses had come in, but it was only myself and a heavenly host of angels.

Curt and I bought a winter home in Tucson. While living there, we went on a vacation with friends, Ken and Donna, to Sedona, AZ. There are beautiful colors of monuments in various shapes and sizes. Shapes such as a bell-shaped tea-pot, etc. We got a map and took off to see them all. Stopped at this one spot, Curt and Donna got out and started up the hill. I soon got out with Ken. When I opened the door, the sky looked eerie like during an eclipse. It was a bluish shade and when I looked down, all the rocks were blue as well as my hands and arms! Running up the hill I was so wound up and chattering like a magpie! Curt looked at me. "I'm blue! I'm blue," I said. I was so energized that I felt like the Energizer bunny and a blue Smurf all in one! As we all came down the hill, I told Donna, "Look at these beautiful blue rocks. I can't believe these rocks are not being sold in stores." So we each picked some up to take home. The next morning after leaving Sedona, I went to get my pretty blue rocks and I was so shocked! They were plain old brown rocks. I could not believe it!

We stopped in the town of Sedona afterwards and while in a store I overheard a clerk talking to a shopper about the vortexes. People would come for spiritual reasons to be healed or to be energized. I told the clerk of my experiences.

She told me I had received the gift many cannot attain, being energized. I felt kind of special at her words.

A few years later another trip to Sedona was planned. I was being "bugged" all the way there with "Are you feeling anything yet?"

Shut up!

We found out this was the area of the vortex. So I wanted to walk up to the same area I had before. Totally different day, sunny, and as I walked up the hill, I felt a calmness come over me as I've never felt before. When I got to the top, I almost wept as I felt as if the Holy Spirit was there within me. I stretched out my arms and prayed to our Lord. When finished, I saw a piece of broken and twisted juniper. As I leaned to pick it up, a breeze came upon me and a voice saying, "Do not remove me." And trust me, I did not!

As I stated earlier, Curt had promised to show me the world and that he did. So we started out on all of our journeys. Seems it would be easier to count where we have not been compared to where we have been. I have so many pictures and albums of our travels to look at when I can no longer travel.

When I was young, I would look at *National Geographic* magazines every chance I got. I loved looking at all the places in the world, wishing to see it all, even the pyramids someday. And little did I know, that would become a reality. God is good.

Some of my favorite adventures are as follows: Poland, climbing the Sydney Bridge in Australia, a Maori Village in New Zealand, southern Africa, riding a camel and seeing the pyramids of Egypt. I have taken a helicopter to the top of a glacier in Alaska and got to go dogsledding.

Our church choir toured Italy and had the opportunity to sing with 500 other voices from around the world. However, we all got to sing one song for the Pope. When the Pope passed by me, he saw all my fingers with rosaries hanging from them. He smiled at me and made the sign of the cross, therefore blessing them.

We performed a concert in Rome. The night of the performance, I couldn't believe how good I sounded. I felt I was singing for the Lord Himself. Hallelujah! I felt I was on a spiritual high. The music was so beautiful and the only way you could hear yourself singing was to cup an ear. I had trouble learning all the pieces of the music because it would be in Latin or another language. Also, I could not read music. The night of the concert, I finally got it all together.

With our little choir, we got to sing in a lot of small churches and cathedrals. One cathedral we sang in was a beautiful Catholic church. No one was there, but we got permission from the priest to practice there and use the organ. We started to sing and honest to God, we sounded like a choir of angels. People outside started coming in to listen as well as some priests to hear us. I have never felt such happiness and love.

I've been to the Holy Land and to most of the places the Bible spoke of (Garden of Gethsemane, Jordan River, Bethlehem, Nazareth, Jerusalem) what a spiritual experience to walk where our Lord walked! We waded in the Jordan River up to our ankles, such a holy feeling there, it was beautiful. I was almost brought to tears several times.

We went to the home of Mary, the mother of Jesus, in Ephesus (Turkey) where she lived out her final days. We went into her home. It was very small, but the holiness felt there was overwhelming for me. I felt so much peace while inside her home. We sampled food from the time of Jesus. There was a fountain outside that had always been there. It has been used continuously since Jesus' time and provided a constant source of holy water. We filled our water bottles with it and have used it at times for various reasons. I still have a very small amount left. Saying the Hail Mary is still a part of my prayers today. Outside there was a small mass going on beside her home. Time came for communion and I knew I couldn't partake as I hadn't made my first communion. But I wanted to so badly. A voice in my head said, "Do it, take it." I felt so relieved as I knew God had given me permission to do so. It was the first and the last time I ever did communion in a Catholic church.

Holy Water

Since returning home I have put holy water on family and friends. Sometimes remarkable results have happened. I would put a drop on their forehead and make the sign of the cross. We would pray, and then all would say the Lord's Prayer.

I have never felt I was a healer by any means, but perhaps just important to do this. I really felt it was needed to do what was my calling.

All of my children and grandchildren have been blessed with some of the same water and some have been blessed with spiritual feelings. I am happy about this and feel it will be passed on. I guess some people pick up on certain vibes and recognize it. Through it all, the good Lord has been by my side forever. My life has been very unusual, unstable, fearful at times, and sad. But I have come through it all, a little better person I hope.

Some ill friends have asked me to put holy water on them and I have. One occasion was with my friend, Nancy. She had hip surgery on one hip and all went well. The second hip surgery didn't go as well. Another surgery was required because of continuous infection. So she was sent to Mayo to seek help. It was decided she would have to undergo a procedure in which she would be bedridden for a couple months. A couple days before this procedure, I asked her to come to my home. I made the sign of the cross on her forehead with the holy water. We prayed and said the Lord's Prayer.

She went in for the surgery and I sat with her daughter. The doctor came out sooner than we expected. We thought something was wrong, The doctor said, "I can't believe it. There isn't any infection present!" I said, "I know why. It was because I put holy water on her! " I explained what it was. He said that sometimes miracles are more effective than medical intervention!

Nancy was to be discharged a couple days later. The doctor told her to stick with the lady with the holy water!

I sent some holy water to my friend, Kathy, in Tucson, Arizona upon hearing of her six-year-old grandson's cancer. Kathy is a devout Catholic and believes in miracles as I do.

She put some on him, prayed and it worked! He is cancer-free and sixteen years old now. A couple of years later his brother who was also six years old developed another form of cancer. Same scenario and he is also cancer free and fourteen years old now. God blessed these two boys and their family.

My friend Kathy and her husband, Bill, had always wanted to come to Bellevue to visit us. Bill had developed a non-cancerous brain tumor which caused him many problems. The doctors weren't quite sure how to treat this tumor.

So they came to visit, hoping the holy water would help him. But when I first saw him, I just knew it was not to be. I later told Kathy that. When I put holy water on him I prayed for the doctors to find an answer for him.

Later the doctors tried to help him but his physical abilities worsened. He later died of an accident. Perhaps God was sparing him of a worse outcome. Bill was a cowboy, a gentleman, and he enjoyed hunting. I loved his gravelly voice and his blue eyes. He always wore boots and a hat and always had a dog at his side. RIP, Bill.

Others I have sent holy water include several with breast cancer. They have all survived.

Our friend, Chuck, asked me to put holy water on him. He had developed prostate cancer and would have to undergo some treatments. Chuck and his wife, Sheri, came over and I placed some on his forehead in the form of a cross. I prayed and then we all said the Lord's Prayer. His cancer needed no treatment afterwards and he has lived cancer-free for six years. However, it has returned within the past six months. But Chuck is doing very well now.

I do not profess to be a healer of any sort. Our Lord has used me in various situations to do His will. I feel blessed and will continue to do His will in whatever form He asks.

And I Kissed the Ground (Poland)

One of my favorite trips was to Poland. My father's parents came from there in the 1900s. I had always wondered if I still had some relatives living there.

So we planned a trip starting with Warsaw and traveling south by motorcoach. Amanda, a granddaughter of Curt's, helped me look for some of my family on the internet. We didn't have a lot of information to go on, but somehow, two weeks before my travels, I got a message from a man named Jarek Stanek. He asked who I was looking for. So I gave him some names of my Polish family and found out we had the same grandmother. I was so excited when I found they lived in a little town about a two hour drive from where we would be spending the night in Krakow. Our motorcoach ride took us to to Krakow, the southern part of Poland. Talk about luck! I hired a driver who could speak English and had a car. He would drive us to my cousin's home in Wola Debowiecka. I could hardly wait!

Going to Poland was a lifelong dream and I always said if I ever get to Poland, my homeland, I would kiss the ground. And that I did. As soon as I hugged my family, I dropped to my knees, thanked God and kissed the ground. I like to think that was another miracle.

Jarek was working in Paris at that time, so I did not get to meet him. But I met my cousin Zbigniew and his wife Wanda, and Jarek's wife, Marta. They had prepared a wonderful meal for my husband, our driver, and myself. A lovely table was set with potatoes, the most delicious perogies I had ever had, and a Polish pork tenderloin. We had wonderful pastries and drank cherry juice.

Our conversation was fun to say the least. We would laugh when we understood what was being said. So our driver would interpret for us, telling us what had been said.

They took us to see where my great-grandparents were married and buried. I noticed all the graves had lots of flowers on them. One of their customs is to decorate the graves as much as possible. The little town was so charming and lovely. My cousin proudly showed us his shed and tractor. Wanda and Marta showed us the canned goods they prepared. We exchanged gifts and it was time to leave. It was so bittersweet; I didn't want to quit hugging. As we started out the driveway, I was crying so hard, I asked to stop and I ran back to hug my cousin once again.

Jarek and Marta have two sons in college. Jarek's brother, Pawel, has a wonderful photography hobby. We send photos to one another. What gift of love to have met my Polish family. Thank you Jesus for a wonderful trip.

Stanek Family
Back Row L-R: Maciej, Jaroslaw, Marta, Karolina Ryba,
Elzbieta Ryba, Ewelina Ryba, Dominik
Front Row L-R: Wanda, Zbigniew

Floral photographs are taken by cousin Pawel Stanek.

I am here, I am blessed (Nebraska)

We've had several vacation homes in Tucson, Arizona. Six to be exact. Must be my mother's blood in me. We spent as much as three months there in the winter. We golfed, hiked, spent time at the pool, ate great food, watched melodramas, had visitors, and the list goes on. After driving back and forth for twenty-two years (Bellevue to Tucson) it started becoming harder to do. Driving through fire areas, tornadoes, icy roads, and snowstorms which caused a night's stay in an armory after being stuck on the interstate for twelve hours. So we've had enough of that kind of adventure to last us a lifetime.

We've seen so much in Arizona and have done everything we wanted to do. I loved it and the mountains, cactus, great Mexican food, and the beautiful sunsets.

Our health and lack of energy made us decide to sell our Arizona home. I suffered a couple of mild strokes, which took a toll. But I recovered very well, thank God. Curt has had some heart issues, so we were ready to slow down.

Our life now is enjoying family and friends, get togethers, some golf, traveling, reading, movies, and napping. We enjoy a good glass of wine or beer, and ice cream. Curt still works part time as a broker at his real estate company. I have started writing poems, reading, and enjoy coloring books for adults. However, my daughter Lyn calls it art.

Cyndi, my oldest, keeps care of my health and medical problems and explains them to me. She works as a head nurse in Pender, Nebraska. She and her family come and spend the night with me whenever possible.

Julie, my second daughter, drives from Blair where she lives and comes once a week to take me around for groceries, just plain shopping and other little jobs I might have for her. She is retired now and takes care of my financial affairs.

Lyn, my youngest daughter, is my spiritual advisor. She lifts me up when I need a boost about our Lord and my life. She lives close to me and I get to see her and her family fairly often. She will take care of my funeral arrangements.

I've asked them all to make me laugh and in my casket to pluck off any chin whiskers I might have.

Miracles

My most recent miracle began with writing this book. I started writing on July 3, 2021. It all began with a UTI.

The pain that I was experiencing became worse the next day, but because of the holiday, the doctor's office was closed. Bad night, up and down, crying with pain, did not want to go to the ER with a UTI. Can you imagine, with all those receiving emergency treatment and there I was, with a UTI!

I had Curt get me some over-the-counter medicine but it didn't help. I could tell my kidneys were starting to hurt worse. I was in a lot of hurt with both bladder and kidneys in pain.

Finally, I was able to see my doctor and got some medication. However, it didn't help very much either. That night, laying on the couch, I felt the room was again full of people and/or angels. They were walking around me with their heads down as if they were praying and I had the sensation of being surrounded by many. So I felt they were there to take me to Heaven. I prayed, "Lord, I am ready if this is my time."

The next morning my daughter Julie took me to the ER and I was admitted to the hospital with a bad case of a UTI, kidney and lung problems, and dehydration. I was in a lot of pain. It was hard to walk unless I had a walker and was held by a belt around my waist. My oxygen level was low and so I had to have oxygen.

Needless to say I was pretty sick that night as I laid there in the hospital room. It felt full of people. I felt a touch on my left calf, one on my thigh, on my right calf, one on my shoulder and the palm of a hand slipped under my right shoulder. Seemed like this was being done by four or five people. I didn't see anybody and I couldn't make out any forms or faces. I believe that it may have been my deceased husband, mother, brother, and sister.

Again I told God, "I'm ready if this is my time, but if not, I desperately need to know what you want me to do. What do I need to get done?"

The next morning, I asked the doctor when I could go home. He told me not for a while, but I would probably have to go to a nursing home for therapy. I wasn't happy about that, but I had no choice. He said I had acute kidney infection and the lower part of my lungs was closing down. I needed more oxygen and he wanted to do a test on me that night while I slept. He said my oxygen level was so low during the day, they wanted to do monitor me closer at night and during my sleep.

I was sitting up when at 10:00 pm a machine was brought in and attached to me. At that time, I was no longer on pain medicine as my pain was gone, but continued on an antibiotic. I asked if this machine had a camera in it, but they said no. It would only tell them my oxygen levels. I could see some bright little light off to the left of the machine. Pointing towards the wall, I asked the nurses if they could see that. They said no. So I told one nurse to come over to my side and to look again, but she still said no. I said thank you and I knew what it was and they left. I was sitting up in bed and no sooner as they closed the door, my miracle began.

The room lit up with multiple, gold, sparkling, moving lights. They were very small, like fairy lights, but so many and they were in constant motion making such beautiful designs I had never seen before. I could see colors of gold unimaginable and designs not earthly.

The colors were unbelievable and I was mesmerized by them all. The patterns were so different than I had ever seen before, very unique. One on the left was like a tornado funnel on its side, the best I could describe it. The whole thing was rotating, like 3-D. I could see it moving and could look right through it. All of these patterns/designs were as large as the wall in front of my bed. The entire wall was filled with lights and was moving. To my left, it looked like windmill fan blades moving around and around.

Both my hands were under the covers, so I took out my left arm. I raised it up and the one from the left side came and started twirling around my arm again and again. Then I did the right arm and the one on the right, twirled around it also. This happened two times. Don't know why I never said anything, I was just so awed by it and felt so calm. Decided to close my eyes for a minute or two to see if it stayed and it did. I knew I was supposed to be sleeping for this test; however, I knew it would be gone when I awoke.

Kitty's First Words from Hospital Bed

~~First word~~ at the end of my bed I began to see beautiful moving gold lights in various designs. I was mesmerized by the scene set before me. The colors + the designs so different were nothing I have ever seen before.

Somehow I knew God had a purpose for me and my remaining days on this earth. So again I prayed, "Please Father, I need to know what you want me to do." I fell asleep and of course when I awoke, my beautiful miracle was gone. Only the memory remained. I couldn't believe it. I felt so wonderful. I could walk without help. I could hold a glass of water. I was smiling remembering what had happened. I fixed my hair, put on makeup, and was ready to go home. I felt better than I had in years!

The doctor came in later and couldn't believe how much I had changed. He told me I did not have to have therapy and could go home the following day.

One of the nurses came in and told me that they didn't think I'd make it through the night. Later on that night I lay praying and received my message. It came to me just like Jesus talking to me. "Go tell your story of miracles. Don't stay quiet. Write it down, talk to friends and strangers. They need to know there is indeed a Heaven."

And I am doing just that. I hit the ground running, sharing my story with all who want to hear about my testimony. I'm still doing this as often as I can.

After my hospital miracle, I have talked with my pastor, a priest, and a spiritualist. How uncanny, all have told me pretty much the same, it is unbelievable. I thought they might think I had made this all up. Not so, thank you Jesus. They all believed me. I asked, why me? And they asked, why not? Why not you and said that remember, Mary was an ordinary woman also. They felt I was blessed and I was able to pick up on different spiritual planes that other people cannot so that I can see, feel, and share my experiences.

Since my last miracle a sense of urgency has come over me. I need to forgive some of my family members. It is a debt I need to forgive.

After a few years of strained and difficult relationships, I was told to humble myself and make amends and ask for their forgiveness. I did just that. Now a feeling of peace and happiness has replaced my anger. Jesus said to forgive others as He has forgiven us. Thank you my Lord for reminding me of these words You spoke!

Some of my children and grandchildren have had unusual experiences as well, especially after Jerry's death.

***

Cyndi - Overwhelming sadness during the month of his death.

Julie - Many experiences she does not want to share publicly.

Lyn - Seeing Jerry in her yard

Kellen - Jerry coming to his bed to comfort him. Jen, his wife also experienced this. Kellen experienced frequent recurring visits

Klint - He would talk to the pull toy as though it were Jerry

Kyle - After Jerry's death, he was frightened by his appearing. I asked Jerry not to visit him.

Jillian - Smelling Jerry's tobacco

Erin - She was born after Jerry's death, but yet as a baby, she could identify his picture and called him "Papa."

Myself - many dreams of him each week since his death. I have felt his touch and heard his voice and understood his words in my mind. Not that long ago, I was awakened by Jerry by my bed. He was smiling and looked so happy and healthy. I sain, "Oh, Jerry!" I reached out to touch him and he was gone. I feel he was letting me know not to be afraid. This was the first time I had seen him. Truly, there is a heaven!

Children, Grands, Greats (Nebraska)

Children	Cyndi	Julie	Lyn
Spouses	Greg	Jim	Brian
Grandchildren and Spouses	Kellen (Jen) Kyle (Kayla) Klint (Kaitlyn)	Jillian (Brad)	Erin (Britain)
Great-Grandchildren	Peyton, Carson, Christian, Archer, & Knox	Benjamin	

Son-in-law, Greg, and daughter, Cyndi

Grandson Kellen, great-grandson Peyton, wife Jen, and great-grandson Carson.

Grandson Kyle, wife Kayla, Great-grandsons Knox, Christian, Archer

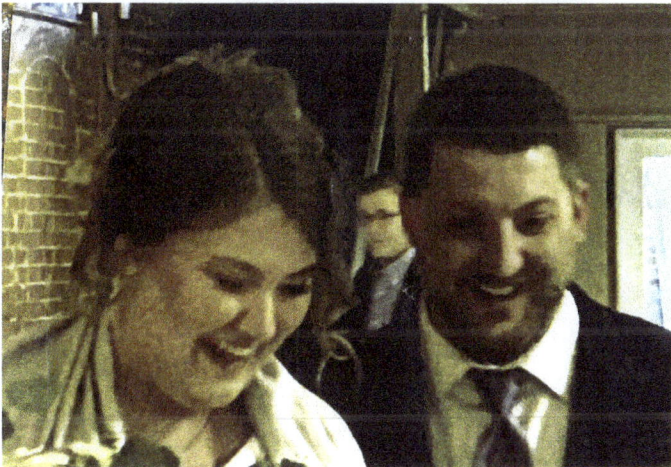

Wife Kaitlyn and grandson Klint

Son-in-law Jim, daughter Julie

Granddaughter Jillian, Great-grandson Benjamin, husband Brad

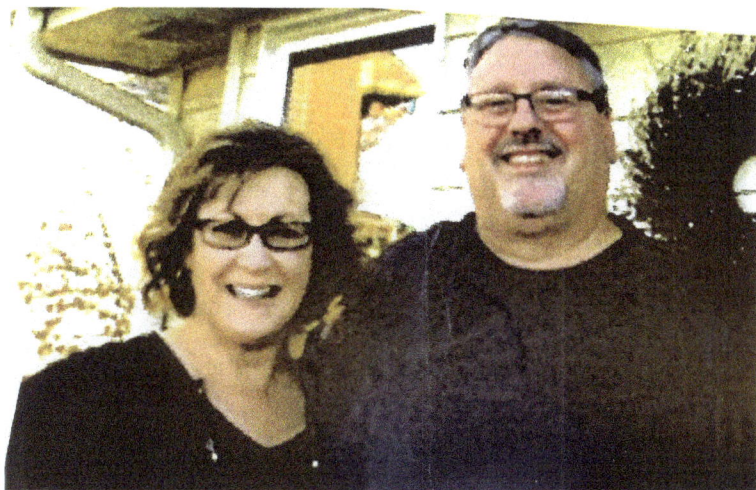

Daughter Lyn and Son-in-law Brian

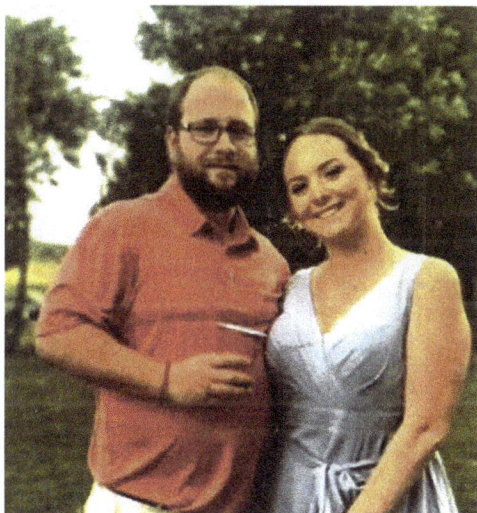

Husband Britain, Granddaughter Erin

My Brothers and Sisters

My sisters and brothers, Jan, Denny, Lela, Shirlee, Nancy, and Dave have played an important role in my life.

When I was little, I thought my brother, Denny, was so handsome. I thought he could be a movie star! He always knew how to manipulate his sisters. He is now in heaven.

Shirlee had huge gardens and did lots of freezing and canning. She was very pretty. I spent some summers with her and she made me a dress.

Nancy, the spunkiest of all. Fun-loving, nice alto voice, good artist, free spirit.

Jan has been my protector. We sometimes laughed in church, even once at a funeral. But we pretended we were crying. We were partners in crime. She could be hurt easily.

My brother, Dave, loved Boy Scouts, horses, and was a gun enthusiast. He loved to tell jokes! He became a minister.

Lela (now in heaven) was my baby sister. She had a nice belly laugh and had a beatiful smile. She loved making craft projects.

Mom, Ruby. Loved us all. Worked very hard for us kids. Could sing, yodel, and always wanted a hug.

Siblings, Jan, Dave, Nancy, and Shirlee

Brother Denny, in Heaven

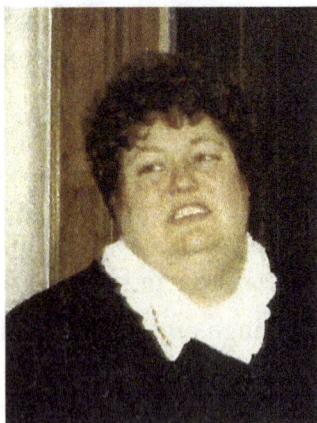

Sister Lela, in Heaven

Spending time with my sisters and brothers in our later years has truly been a blessing. Reminiscing our childhood years and growing up together, telling the same stories over and over, and embellishing them every time. Our bouts of laughing until we cried and having a margarita or glass of wine is always our scenario.

Each of us is trying to outdo each other. There were always Polish Poker and Oh Shoot card games. Winning a few extra quarters was always a perk. Our experiences have been from visiting our childhood homes and churches to dressing up silly with goofy hats and black electrical tape on our eyebrows and for a mustache. My niece and I would dance and sing for them. We were pretty awful, but they loved it. We loved our Mexican and Polish food and made some of our mother's recipes. We are all from different states: Minnesota, California, New Mexico, and Nebraska. And we each have had a time to host our sister's getaway. Someday we will be too old to travel or have passed on, but for now, party on.

Another fun experience could have been out of a scene from the *Golden Girls*. All four of us resemble one of them. At this time, we happened to be at my sister Jan's home. We had been invited to her daughter and son-in-law's home for dinner. I drove my sister Jan's car.

After eating, we all had a small glass of Polish wine that I had brought back from Poland. We toasted our family, the Staneks, who live there. Then it was time to go and we took the rest of the wine with us and drove to Jan's place a few blocks from her daughter's home. We got in the car and started down the street and noticed no head lights. "OK, Jan, where are the lights? My lights automatically come on." She said, "I don't know, I've never driven it at night." I couldn't find how to turn them on, but did find that if I held the turn signal up, we had lights. So away we went. A couple blocks to the highway and then a right to Jan's home.

When we went to get on the highway, we looked for any cops or cars and waited until no cars were coming. OK, safe to go. We no more than got on the highway until I said, "Is that blue lights flashing behind me?" "Yes, they shouted." So I pulled over and here come three policemen our way. I look back and Shirley looked like she was praying, Nancy looking innocent and hiding the Polish wine was staring straight ahead.

Flashlights were all over us. My sister Jan, beside me, was almost in tears and shaking trying to find her registration in the glove box. I couldn't get the window down so I had to open the door. Why I couldn't, I don't know. I was more upset about maybe getting a ticket as I have never had one to this day.

Jan nearly broke into tears, saying "I've never been stopped before by an officer, I'm so sorry." The officer said, "Do you know why I stopped you?" I replied, "No." He said, "You have no taillights." He showed me how to turn the lights on and no ticket thank God but he followed us for quite a while. I'm sure the police officers had a good laugh about stopping four old ladies.

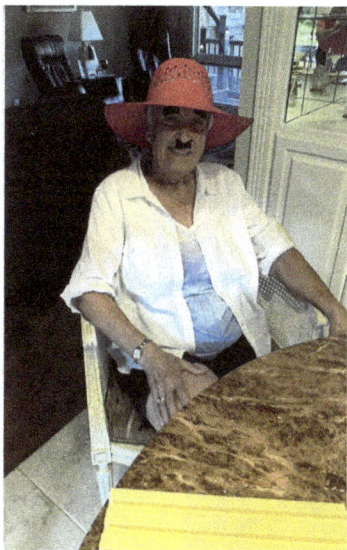

Shirlee

Nancy

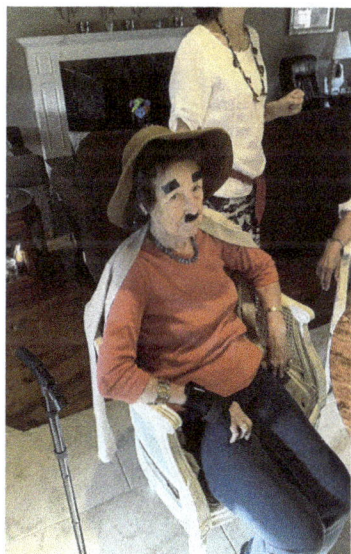

Jan

Kathy

Yours truly, totally normal

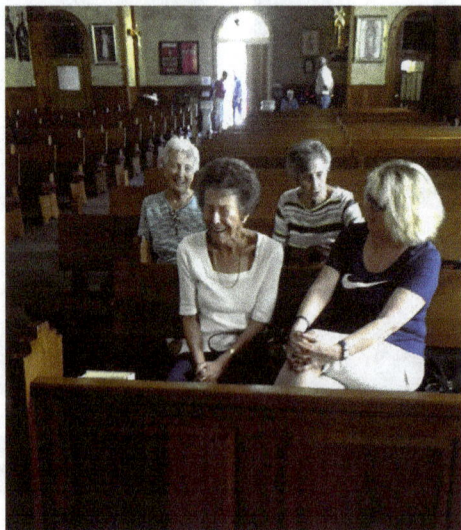

Giggling in church and getting scolded.

Appendix A: Facts About Me, My Life

- Moves
  - 31
    - Minnesota, Wyoming, Idaho, Iowa, & Nebraska
    - Minnesota - St. Peter & Minneapolis
    - Wyoming - Casper
    - Idaho - Salmon & Mackey
    - Iowa - Carter Lake, Pisgah & Mondamin
    - Nebraska - Omaha, Bellevue
- Schools
  - 12
    - K - Minnesota
    - 1st - 4th Grade: Wyoming
    - 5th Grade: Nebraska
    - 6th Grade: Idaho
    - 7th - 8th Grade: Iowa & Nebraska
    - 9-12th Grade: Iowa & Nebraska
- Horses, Cats, Dogs (And I remember all their names!)

- Places I've Been
  - United States
    - Alaska, Hawaii,
  - Abroad
    - Poland, Sweden, Finland, Norway, Russia, Switzerland, Austria, Italy, France, Scotland, England, Germany, Spain, Mexico, Egypt, Israel, Turkey, Czechoslovakia, Australia, Canada, Bermuda, Bahamas, Caribbean (Eastern/ Western) New Zealand, Honduras, South Africa.
- Collections.
  - more than thirty angels
  - crosses
  - rosaries

- Katherine Helena Pekula (Kitty)

  - Mother - Nancy Carolyn (Ruby) Marcum

  - Maternal Grandmother & Grandfather - Martha Missouri Grimes & Rubin Marcum

  - Maternal Great-Grandmother & Great-Grandfather - Letta Clark & William Grimes

  - Father - Edward Pekula

  - Paternal Grandmother & Grandfather - Katherine Knitter & Andrew Pekula

  - Paternal Great-Grandmother and Great-Grandfather - Josephine Stanek and Simon Pekula

- Jerry Lynn Carrier

- Mother - Juanita Lightwine

- Father - Fred Carrier

- Maternal Grandmother - Toni Straight

- Maternal Grandfather - Steve Lightwine

116

My Closing Thoughts

Looking back over the years with Jerry, my first love, I wish things could have been different. I should have opened up to Jesus, and I didn't . I have made many mistakes, and feel Jerry couldn't help his behavior at times. I would have lived with him forever. He has left three children and their spouses, five grandchildren and their spouses, some he never met, and seven great-grandchildren at this time. I've had so many happy memories with Jerry

Thinking back, I never really openly discussed my spirituality. I said my prayers, went to church, but never had conversations about God. How sad was that! I don't know why I didn't. I never attended Bible Study or prayer groups. Very odd now that I think about that. I have felt the Lord's touch and I have also heard His voice in my mind. Guess I felt it was my own personal connection with God.

Curt has been a good husband and is good to my children. Currently, he still works at his office and enjoys golf and Nebraska football. We have been married for twenty-two years.

My life has slowed down and I love getting together with my family and friends. Traveling still ranks high on my list of activities as well as writing, reading, movies, music, and coloring books for adults.

I no longer feel guilty about sleeping late or napping, finally! I don't mind being in my pajamas by 7:00 in the evening! Having a nice glass of wine sitting in my recliner with my kitty Meiko on my lap is about as good as it gets!

I will still give testimony to everyone I can. My Lord has blessed me and given me a mission to fulfill. I'll do my best! I am on the threshold of heaven!

Kitty's Special Thank Yous

Thank you to my oldest grandson, Kellen. He listened to me read to him from my longhand writing. I kept pausing to ask him, "Does this sound OK?"

He always replied, "It's your story Grandma." He put my words into his computer and made all of it come alive for me.

To Ruth Tempelmann, Ph.D., my editor and friend. You made me feel like my story was worth telling. Thank you for all your patience and encouragement. Your expertise, knowledge, and inspiration made me realize my dream!